OFFICE OF THE CHIEF OF PUBLIC AFFAIRS

THE UNITED STATES ARMY
SOCIAL MEDIA
HANDBOOK
VERSION 2 | AUGUST 2011

ONLINE AND SOCIAL MEDIA DIVISION | 1500 PENTAGON | WASHINGTON, DC

U.S. ARMY

▼ Optimizing Online Engagement

Army
Social
Media

Table of Contents

Letter from the Chief of Public Affairs II

Social media summary 1

Social media for Soldiers and Army personnel. 2

Social media standards for Army leaders 3

OPSEC and safe social networking 4

Establishing and maintaining Army social media presences. 6

Using social media for crisis communications 8

Checklists for establishing an official Army social media presence 10

Army branding 12

Blogging 13

Social media impersonations. 14

Social media case studies. 15

Facebook quick reference guide. 20

Twitter quick reference guide. 21

Frequently asked questions. 22

Official Army social media presences 24

Social media resources. 25

Social media glossary. 26

Enclosure (1) Department of the Army Standard Operating Procedure
    Standardizing Official U.S. Army External Presences (Social Media) 36

Enclosure (2) Department of the Army Delegation of Authority
    Approval of External Official Presences 38

Enclosure (3) Directive-Type Memorandum (DTM) 09-026
    Responsible and Effective Use of Internet-based Capabilities 40

Letter from the Chief of Public Affairs

Team,

I want to recognize and applaud all the great work each of you are doing to help the Army tell our story.

As communicators, we operate in a 24-hour news cycle with the news moving faster than ever before. In order to be successful at telling the Army's story, we must take full advantage of all the communication tools at our disposal.

It is important to be as transparent as possible. As communicators, we need to be the first with the truth, whether it's good or bad. Social media allows us to do that while also painting a visual picture which allows us to shape messages.

Recently, Army organizations have used social media to communicate during times of crisis. Communications regarding the earthquake in Japan, the tsunami threat in Hawaii, the tornadoes and floods in the Midwest - all benefited from Army communicators turning to social media to inform and update the public and the community.

In today's media environment, understanding social media, especially as it relates to time, can help you excel as an Army communicator. People expect news to find them through social media platforms, so when breaking news happens, one of the first places they turn is social media. Social media can be a valuable tool for Army organizations. It helps Army organizations and Army commands establish credibility, accessibility and authenticity.

In this edition of the Social Media Handbook, we have included updates to Army social media policy and new examples of Army leaders using social media effectively. We provided instructions on how to respond to social media imposters and fake sites. We have also included an expanded operations security section and added an extensive social media glossary.

Social media is constantly evolving, and it is not going away. Soldiers have always been and always will be our best story tellers – they are the Strength of the Nation. Social media helps us connect America to its Army and assists us in reaching new demographics.

Best of luck with your social media endeavors. We look forward to working with all of you as we continue to improve the way we tell the Army's story through social media. Please reach out to our Online and Social Media Division if you need any assistance.

STEPHEN R. LANZA
Major General, USA
Chief of Public Affairs

Social Media Summary

What is social media?

Social media represents a shift in the way we as a culture communicate. By using Internet-based platforms like Facebook, Twitter, Flickr and You-Tube, social media provides new ways to connect, interact and learn. People no longer look for news; the news find them. And in the world of social media, the perception of truth can be just as powerful as the truth itself. The Internet moves information quickly, whether for good or bad. Social media, with a variety of available platforms, can instantaneously connect users within a global network, making the transfer of information even more pervasive. Today, social media use is so widespread and transparent that you may already be involved even if you are not actively participating. It is a highly effective tool for reaching large communities and audiences. But this substantial ability to connect with the masses is not without its risks. Using social media to spread information is becoming the standard, so it is important to understand the power, the benefits and the risks associated with using the various platforms.

Army social media

The Army recognizes that social media gives people the ability to communicate with larger audiences faster and in new ways. It has become an important tool for Army messaging and outreach. The Army uses a variety of social media platforms designed to support a range of media from text, audio, pictures and videos; all of which are generated and maintained by organizations and individuals within the Army Family. The Army understands the risks associated with social media and has developed training to help Soldiers and Family members use social media responsibly (www. slideshare.net/USArmySocialMedia).

Why use social media?

Soldiers have always been the Army's best and most effective messengers. Today, Army social media enables the Army Family around town, around the country and around the world to stay connected and spread the Army's key themes and messages. Every time a member of the Army Family joins Army social media, it increases the timely and transparent dissemination of information. It ensures that the Army's story is shared honestly and directly to Americans where they are and whenever they want to see, read or hear it. Social media allows every Soldier to be a part of the Army story and it allows America to connect with its Army. Social media is a cheap, effective and measurable form of communication. The Army uses social media to tell the Army's story, but it also uses social media to listen.

What does the DoD say about social media?

On February 25, 2010, the DoD re-issued a Directive-Type Memorandum providing guidelines for military use of social media and acknowledged "that Internet-based capabilities are integral to operations across the Department of Defense." On March 1, 2011, William J. Lynn III, the Deputy Secretary of Defense, reauthorized Directive-Type Memorandum (DTM) 09-026 – Responsible and Effective Use of Internet-based Capabilities (Enclosure 3). The move extends the DTM through January 2012 and outlines how the NIPRNET should be configured to allow access to Internet-based capabilities across all DoD components. All service branches are using social media at different levels, but this DTM indicates that use of social media in the DoD is authorized. The extension is not a permanent solution, but it allows the military to continue using social media until a more permanent list of rules and regulations is established.

The way forward

The Office of the Assistant Secretary of Defense is currently working on all-encompassing policy including data points currently listed in DTM 09-026 as well as updates to the DoD's 1998 web policy. The DoD instruction is in the creation stage since this policy is presently in draft form. Once vetted and approved, the instruction will be a compendium of everything that will be needed for use of Internet-based capabilities – to include content on ethics, operations security and information assurance. Once published, it will be posted on the Army's SlideShare site.

Social Media for Soldiers and Army Personnel

Joining social networks

Soldiers will naturally seek out involvement in social media platforms if they haven't already. Social media helps individuals with similar interests connect and interact. Soldiers are authorized to use and belong to a variety of social media platforms as long as their involvement does not violate unit policy and the basic guidelines of the Uniform Code of Military Justice.

Lay out the guidelines

All leaders should communicate social media expectations with their Soldiers. It is important to outline unit policy and make sure all Soldiers know what they can and cannot do when using various social media platforms. A generic unit policy can be found on the Army's SlideShare site and it can be customized to each unit.

Follow the Uniform Code of Military Justice

Soldiers using social media must abide by the Uniform Code of Military Justice (UCMJ) at all times. Commenting, posting or linking to material that violates the UCMJ or basic rules of Soldier conduct is prohibited. Social media provides the opportunity for Soldiers to speak freely about their activities and interests. However, Soldiers are subject to UCMJ even when off duty, so talking negatively about supervisors or releasing sensitive information is punishable under the UCMJ. It is important that all Soldiers know that once they log on to a social media platform, they still represent the Army.

Security items to consider

- Look closely at all privacy settings. Set security options to allow visibility to "friends only."

- Do not reveal sensitive information about yourself such as schedules and event locations.

- Ask, "What could the wrong person do with this information?" and "Could it compromise the safety of myself, my family or my unit?"

- Geotagging is a feature that reveals your location to other people within your network. Consider turning off the GPS function of your smartphone and digital camera.

- Photos and videos can go viral quickly. Closely review them before posting to ensure they don't give away sensitive information which could be dangerous if released.

- Talk to your family about operations security. Be sure they know what can and cannot be posted.

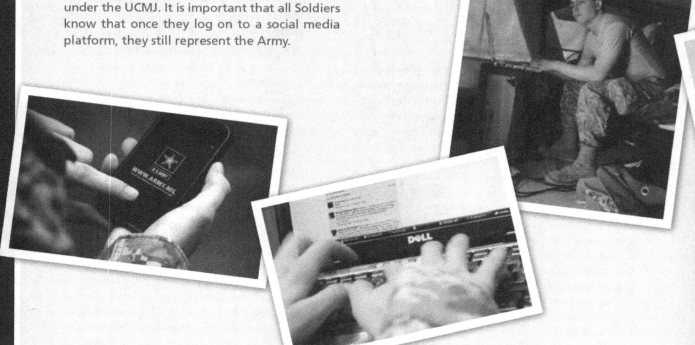

Social Media Standards for Army Leaders

Social media for leaders

Social media has improved the way we communicate, but social media use can present some challenges for leaders.

Online relationships

Social media is about connecting, so it is only natural that Army leaders may interact and function in the same social media spaces as their subordinates. How they connect and interact with their subordinates online is left to their discretion, but it is advised that the online relationship function in the same manner as the professional relationship.

Should Soldiers "follow" those in their command?

This is also left to the discretion of the Army leader. Ultimately, it depends on how that leader uses social media. If the leader is using social media as a way to receive command and unit information along with installation updates, then following members in a leader's command is appropriate. But if the leader is using social media as a way to keep in touch with family and friends, it may not make sense to follow people in the leader's chain of command. Leaders cannot require that members of their unit accept a friend request from their personal profile account.

Leader conduct online

When in a position of leadership, conduct online should be professional. By using social media, leaders are essentially providing a permanent record of what they say. If you would not say it in front of a formation, do not say it online. If a leader finds evidence of a Soldier violating command policy or the UCMJ on social media platforms, then that leader should respond in the same manner they would if they witnessed the infraction in any other environment.

Self promotion

Using rank, job, and/or responsibilities in order to promote oneself online for personal or financial gain is not appropriate. Such actions can damage the image of the Army and an individual command.

Paid submissions

Treat requests from non-governmental blogs for a blog post as a media request and coordinate with your public affairs officer. It is against Army regulations to accept compensation for such posts.

OPSEC and Safe Social Networking

Safe social networking

Social media has become a big part of our Army lives. It helps organizations share information and keeps Soldiers, Family members and Army Civilians connected to loved ones. We depend on social media, but it can be extremely dangerous if you are not careful. Do you know what information you can post about your job? Did you know people can use social media to steal your identity? Did you know you can be at risk, even if you don't use social media? Operations security (OPSEC) and personal privacy concerns should be paramount when using social media.

OPSEC in daily interactions

Sites like Facebook, Twitter, YouTube and Flickr are becoming more important in day-to-day interactions. Since social media use is so commonplace, it is easy to become complacent when using the platforms. But in order to maintain OPSEC, it is important to remain vigilant at all times. Sharing seemingly trivial information online can be dangerous to loved ones and fellow Soldiers in the unit—and may even get them killed. America's enemies scour blogs, forums, chat rooms and personal websites to piece together information that can harm the United States and its Soldiers. Be cautious when accepting friend requests and interacting with people online. You should never accept a friend request from someone you do not know, even if they know a friend of yours. Don't share information that you don't want to become public. Someone might target you based on the fact that you work in the DoD so be cautious when listing your job, military organization, education and contact information. Providing too much information in your profile can leave you exposed to people who want to steal your identity or sensitive operational information.

Privacy settings

Understanding what you can and cannot post on social media platforms goes a long way in protecting yourself online, but more can be done by adjusting your privacy settings. For example, Facebook's default privacy settings are often public, but the platform provides various options that help users adjust and customize their privacy settings. Similarly, Twitter allows users to keep their Tweets private and Flickr gives users the option of keeping photos private. The settings are easily accessible; the trick is setting them to meet your privacy needs.

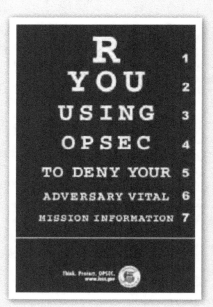

Geotagging safety

Geotagging is the process of adding geographical identification to photographs, video, websites and SMS messages. It is the equivalent of adding a 10-digit grid coordinate to everything you post on the internet. Geotags are sometimes automatically embedded in pictures taken with smartphones, digital cameras, and many people are unaware of the fact that the photos they load to the Internet have been geotagged.

Location-based social networking is quickly growing in popularity. A variety of applications are capitalizing on users' desire to broadcast their geographic location. The increased popularity of these applications is changing the way we, as a digital culture, view security and privacy on an individual level. These changes in perception are also creating OPSEC concerns on an Army level. One Soldier exposing his/her location can affect the entire mission. Deployed Soldiers or Soldiers conducting operations in classified areas should not use location-based social networking services. These services will bring the enemy right to the Army's doorstep.

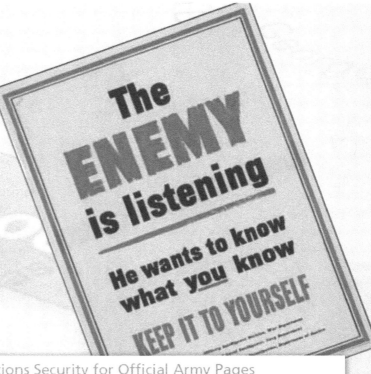

Checklist for Operations Security for Official Army Pages

☐ Designate members of your team responsible for posting content to the official online presence and make sure those individuals are current on all OPSEC training.

☐ Make sure all content is submitted to and approved by the commander or the organization's release authority prior to posting.

☐ Make sure all content is posted in accordance with organization Public Affairs guidance and Army regulations.

☐ Monitor your social media presence and make sure external social media users are not posting sensitive information on your official presence. Monitor your Facebook wall and comments posted to your YouTube, Flickr and Blog presences.

☐ Produce training materials and conduct regular social media OPSEC training within your team and with other units in your organization.

☐ Distribute social media OPSEC training to the families of your Soldiers. It is important to keep them just as informed and up-to-date as the Soldiers in your unit.

☐ Be vigilant. Never become complacent when it comes to OPSEC. Check social media presences within your organization for OPSEC violations. Never stop working to protect OPSEC. Once the information is out there, you can't get it back.

Making Potentially Dangerous Social Media Posts Safer

Dangerous	Safer
My Soldier is in XYZ at ABC Camp in ABC City, Afghanistan.	My Soldier is deployed to Afghanistan.
My Soldier will be leaving Kuwait and heading to Iraq in three days.	My Soldier deployed this week.
My Soldier is coming back at XYZ time on XYZ day.	My Soldier will be home this summer.
My family is back in Edwardsville, IL.	I'm from the Midwest.

Establishing and Maintaining Army Social Media Presences

Managing a social media presence

Today, the Army understands that social media has increased the speed and transparency of information. More Army organizations are using social media for strategic online engagement. Social media is used in garrison environments, operational environments and in Family Readiness Groups. Developing a successful social media presence does not happen overnight. It is a detailed process that requires extensive planning and detailed execution. It all starts with stating the organization's missions, messages and themes.

Developing a strategy

Once an organization establishes a direction, it can begin to develop a social media communication strategy. This strategy must be detailed and provide input into all the social media platforms supported by the organization. The purpose of using social media is to place your unit's messages in the social media space. But in order to keep people coming back to the pages, units should develop a strategy that mixes these messages with items the audience finds interesting. Language should be conversational, fun and engaging. Also, keep in mind that official use of social media platforms must be in compliance with Army public affairs policy. Content must be in the public domain or approved for release by the commanding officer. Commands are ultimately responsible for content posted on their platforms.

Registration

DTM 09-026 requires that all official social media presences be registered with the DoD. Registering the presence indicates that it is official. To register with the Army, visit: www.army.mil/socialmedia. Once a site is approved, it appears on the Army social media directory and is included in any DoD Terms of Service Agreements. Another benefit to registering is that Facebook will remove paid advertisements from all official Army Facebook pages. For more information on the social media approval process, refer to Delegation of Authority – Approval of External Official Presences (Enclosure 2).

Contact information

It is vitally important to provide up-to-date unit contact information on your social media platforms. Facebook pages and YouTube channels are required to provide an AKO email address and a mailing address for the unit. However, since some platforms like Twitter allow less space for this information, it is sufficient to provide just an email address.

Terms of use statement

Each social media presence must have a terms of use statement that informs visitors of what is authorized when interacting on the platform. This terms of use statement should include a general disclaimer, privacy and security disclaimers, a copyright and trademark disclaimer, moderated presence disclaimer and a Freedom of Information Act notice. For an example of a terms of use statement, review the Army's terms of use statement on the Army's official Facebook page: goo.gl/ySaQx.

Enforce posting policy and monitor comments

It is good to have a posting policy, but just because a posting policy is in place does not mean everyone will follow it. Make sure to review wall posts frequently and remove posts that violate the posting policy. Keep in mind that social media doesn't take a break for the weekend. In some instances, weekend activity on Facebook can be busier than the week, so watch the organization's wall every day, even on days off, holidays and weekends.

Engage the audience

Social media is more than just a platform to push command messages; it is a social community. Platforms like Facebook and Twitter help people bridge geographical gaps to connect, talk and interact. Using social media can be valuable to a communication strategy, but it needs to be more than a sounding board for organization messages. Social media should be used to facilitate the conversation, engage the population and keep people interested in the discussion to bring America closer to its Army.

Listen to the audience

By reading the comments on a Facebook wall or blog post, social media managers can get a feel for what the online community wants to hear. It is also useful talk to your audience directly. Ask for feedback and suggestions, and then act on their responses. A social media presence accomplishes very little if the audience is not interested in what is being said.

Mix it up

Balance "fun" with "medicine." It is important to post command messages and organizational information, but try to keep the page entertaining enough for people to want to follow it. Don't be afraid to have fun by posting interesting links or asking trivia questions. Try posting a photo of the day or asking a weekly question. Social media is social, so it is important not to fall into the trap of talking at your audience.

Answer questions

Once a social media presence grows to a certain size, the population will likely use it as a resource and forum to ask questions. It is important to spend time responding to questions to establish a valued relationship with users. The one-on-one conversations will show the community that their voices are being heard.

Measurement

Ten years ago, the success and reach of a news story could be measured by the size of a newspaper's circulation or the number of clicks on a website. Today, measurement is about more than just numbers. It is about trends and human feedback. Social media sites like Facebook, Twitter, Flickr and YouTube provide their own free analytics tools that allow administrators to track views, impressions and comments. By using numbers in conjunction with comments and reader feedback, it is easier than ever to determine how organizational messages are received and how the audience is responding to the content. Some analytics tools provide graphs and charts, but ultimately the presentation of information depends on the platform. These different presentations make for a richer statistical analysis. Using free analytics tools can help a unit demonstrate the usefulness of a social media platform, and even highlight the success of a specific social media campaign.

Using Social Media for Crisis Communications

Promote organizational social media presences

It is important to tell the social media community that you're out there. Attach links to social media platforms at the bottom of press releases and in the signature block of official emails from your office. The more you get the word about out a social media presence, the faster the community that follows it will grow.

Post content to social media platforms often

A static social media presence is ineffective. Static pages are boring and visitors to the page lose interest quickly. If content on the page is not regularly updated, people will stop coming by to view the page. Carefully select links to stories, unit videos and photos related to the organization's mission. Social media platforms are designed to support various forms of content, so take advantage of that. Once information is cleared by a release authority, post it. Social media moves information quicker than ever, so don't wait for a press release. If the information is there and approved for release, use it. This includes information about negative news items, as well.

Build a community

A large social media following doesn't happen over night, so relax and execute the social media strategy. The better an organization is at providing good information and engaging its social media audience, the faster the following will grow.

Crisis management

Using social media to communicate with stakeholders during a crisis has proven to be effective due to its speed, reach and direct access. In recent crises, social media has helped distribute command information to key audiences and media, while also providing a means for dialogue among the affected and interested parties. For a case study on how to use social media in a crisis situation, refer to this Army presentation: goo.gl/4S1HA.

You can't force trust

The best course of action during a crisis is to leverage existing social media presences. It is important to have a regularly updated channel of communication between the organization and key audiences before a crisis hits so they know where to find information online.

Monitor content from users

Monitor content posted by users to get a better understanding of what information they want/need. Staff posts appropriately to answer questions as best as possible. This ensures that your audience knows the organization is listening.

Post cleared information as it comes in

When a crisis hits, there's no need to wait for a formal press release. When you have solid, approved/cleared information that audiences want to know, post it. You can always post updated information as it becomes available. Not posting updates quickly during a crisis, or not keeping the community informed may damage the organization's credibility.

The March 2011 Japan Tsunami is a good example of how the Army successfully used social media to get critical information to key audiences during a crisis.

Use mobile devices

Keep your social media presences up-to-date by using mobile devices, if necessary. The myriad of mobile devices available today allow you to update social sites without being tied to your computer at a desk. Crisis happen all the time, so be prepared. Whether the installation is on lockdown, you're waiting out a storm or you're at a remote site at the scene, mobile devices allow you to share quick updates immediately. Make sure to ensure your mobile devices are continuously charged. Be creative in finding power solutions that work for your situation.

Answer questions

Avoid just posting information on a social media presence. Be prepared to receive questions. Respond back as quickly as possible through the most appropriate means of communication.

Monitor conversations

Listen to what audiences are talking about and be prepared to engage. This is the best way to stop rumors before they run rampant. Use search engines and other monitoring tools to track discussions on various topics.

Share information

Share critical information with a network of trusted social media sites, such as other Army command sites, government and official non-governmental sites like the American Red Cross.

The social media community is large and it is possible to reach a lot of people through an extended network in the social media space.

Encourage people on the scene to send info

Organizations can do this by having individuals on the scene either use their personal accounts or feed you information to post on the official command social sites. No matter how the information is submitted, the command site should promote this content when appropriate. It also helps to follow trends and related pages so your organization can repurpose information when appropriate.

Promote social media presences

Organizations should advertise their social media presences on outgoing press releases, email signatures, links on the home page and in conversations with reporters. The social media presence isn't helpful if people don't know about it. Be aggressive when sending out information and make sure the public knows that the organization's social media presences are a good resource for information.

Analyze results

Once the crisis is over, analyze what happened. Evaluate metrics and track user feedback. It is important to evaluate how a social media presence performs during a crisis so adjustments can be made for the future.

Checklists for Establishing an Official
Army Social Media Presence

PRIOR TO ESTABLISHING AN OFFICIAL SOCIAL MEDIA PRESENCE, CONSIDER THESE ITEMS

☐ **Get command approval -** See Delegation of Authority memo (Enclosure 2).

☐ **Study Army social media policy and read Army resources -** Before you get started with social media, it is important to understand Army social media policy. Army social media resources can be found at: www.slideshare.net/USArmySocialMedia.

☐ **Determine your goals -** What do you want to achieve/communicate? It could include distributing command information, connecting to a community, building espirit de corps, etc.

☐ **Determine your audience -** Identify the audience you intend to communicate with. This can include Soldiers, Families, Veterans, Army Civilians and the general public. Don't forget, your audience will also include stakeholders, politicians, community leaders and adversaries or enemies.

☐ **Research and select social media platforms -** Identify the social media platforms that will best suit the needs of your organization. Not all platforms will work for some organizations, so make sure you understand what can be achieved with each platform. Look at what other organizations are doing to get ideas.

☐ **Select your name and branding -** Read the Army's SOP for social media platforms to get detailed naming and branding procedures (www.slideshare.net/USArmySocialMedia/army-social-media-standard-operating-procedure-standardization). For more information on branding, visit: www.usarmybrandportal.com or www.army.mil/Create.

☐ **Draft content strategy -** After identifying your audiences, selecting the platforms and approving branding, begin drafting a posting strategy. This helps refine your organization's social media goals. For an example of a social media strategy, visit: goo.gl/3Tmw0.

☐ **Determine site management strategy -** Identify social media managers on your team. Make sure contingency plans are in place to allow for other members to fill in on established duties if necessary.

☐ **Develop policies and training -** The social media team is responsible for developing organization-specific social media policies to include posting and commenting policies. Also make sure to develop training materials to help educate and train individuals in your command about social media and its uses. To view the Army's social media training resource, visit: www.slideshare.net/USArmySocialMedia.

REQUIREMENTS FOR AN OFFICIAL PUBLIC FACING COMMAND SOCIAL MEDIA PRESENCE
(THIS MEANS A PUBLIC SITE, NOT ONE BEHIND A FIREWALL)

☐ **Commanding officer or public affairs officer approval** - A presence must be approved by the release authority before it can be registered. Delegation of Authority – Approval of External Official Presences (Enclosure 2).

☐ **The point of contact must include a valid .mil address each time an organization submits for approval.**

☐ **The presence must have a URL to an official Army website** - Your command's website or the Army.mil if your organization does not have a website.

☐ **The presence must post disclaimer text** - The disclaimer identifies the page as an "official" Army social media presence and disclaims any endorsement. An example can be found here: on.fb.me/eulvUR.

☐ **The presence must be clearly identified as "official"** - Site must identify that the presence is "official" somewhere on the page. An example can be found in the left-hand column of the Army's Facebook page: www.facebook.com/USArmy. For an example of how to identify an official Twitter, look at the top of the Army's official Twitter account: www.twitter.com/USArmy.

☐ **The presence must be unlocked and open to the public** - This mostly applies to Twitter, but also means that private Facebook groups should not be registered on the Army's social media directory. All official presences are open to the public.

☐ **Only official presences on Facebook can be registered and should be labeled as "Organization-Government"** - The use of Facebook Profile, Community and Group pages for official purposes violates the government's terms of service agreement with Facebook.

☐ **Submit the social media presence for approval and registration to** www.army.mil/socialmedia.

☐ **Set default view of your Facebook wall to show posts by only your organization.**

☐ **Make sure YouTube channels are set up as a government presence.** Step-by-step instructions can be found at: forum.webcontent.gov/?page=TOS_YouTube.

Army Branding

Using Army branding

A brand is not just a logo or an emblem; it is an organization's identity. When using Army branding on social media sites, it is important to use the correct colors, tagline and imagery. A brand represents the organization through distinctive visual elements, which uphold the integrity of the brand when used consistently and correctly across all communications.

Staying Army Strong

"Army Strong" is a unique brand of strength. Everyone is familiar with the tangible power of the U.S. Army: the Apaches, the Humvees, the weaponry, the pushups. This campaign highlights the true strength of our Army—the strength that lies within each and every Soldier. It is harder to see, but it is this strength that makes the U.S. Army the preeminent land power on earth. Thus, maintaining the same consistent branding across all Army sites (social media or otherwise) is vitally important.

U.S. Army Brand Portal
www.usarmybrandportal.com

The U.S. Army Brand Portal provides brand elements such as Army logos, camouflage backgrounds, color palettes, typography and released Army photography. The site also provides guidelines on how to use those elements together. By getting brand elements and guidelines from the same place, people can ensure their use of Army branding is consistent with the Army's own designs.

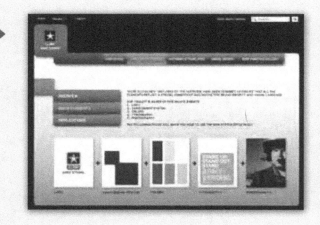

ARMY.MIL CREATE
www.army.mil/create

Creating a unit specific brand while following the Army style can seem overwhelming, but the Army.mil Create website can help get you started. There, you will find Designer, Web Developer and Content Editor tips that guide you through creating your own brand. There is even a social media toolkit your team can download.

Blogging

What is a blog?

A blog (also known as a "web log") is a type of website, usually maintained by an individual with regular entries of commentary, descriptions of events or other material such as video or graphics. Entries are commonly displayed in reverse-chronological order. "Blog" can also be used as a verb, meaning to maintain or add content to a blog. Many blogs provide commentary or news on a particular subject; others function as personal online diaries. A typical blog combines text, images, video and links to other blogs, websites, and related media to its topic. The ability of readers to leave comments in an interactive format is an important part of many blogs. Most blogs are textual, although some focus on art (art blog), photographs (photoblog), videos (video blog), music (MP3 blog), audio (podcast) and microblogging (Twitter).

Army Live Blog
www.army.mil/blog

The U.S. Army's official blog, Army Live, offers Soldiers, Veterans and Families the opportunity to share their experiences with the Army Family on a more personal, informal platform. In addition, it allows the U.S. Army to share information and news that sparks thoughtful and engaging conversations. To submit content for publication on Army Live, send an email to ocpa.osmd@us.army.mil. Be sure to include photographs, graphics and related links to include in the blog post.

Army Strong Stories
www.armystrongstories.com

Army Strong Stories is an Army blog and story-sharing program that provides an online community for Soldiers, Families, friends and supporters to share their Army stories on Army life and military service. Hundreds of Soldiers and supporters submit new video and written stories every day. Army Strong Stories has two main features – the Soldier blog and Army stories. The Soldier blog is exclusive to Soldiers, Cadets, Veterans and Army Civilians, but anyone can share video or written submissions through Army stories.

Social Media Impersonations

Social media impersonations

Occasionally, social media users claim to be someone they are not. This practice can become a problem when users claim to be Army officials or Soldiers. Some individuals impersonate others for recognition, while others do it for financial gain. The practice of impersonating Soldiers for financial gain is common. When imposter accounts are identified, it is important to report the accounts to the host platforms. Twitter allows for imposter accounts, if they indicate that they are "unofficial" or "fan" accounts.

Reporting impersonations

Imposter accounts are violations of terms of use agreements and can be damaging to a Soldier's reputation, as well as the Army. Most social media platforms have a reporting system that allows users to report an individual who is pretending to be someone else. If a high-level Army official, such as a General Officer, is impersonated, contact the Online and Social Media Division at ocpa.osmd@us.army.mil so the situation can be resolved quickly.

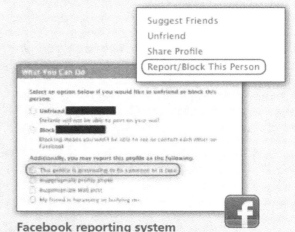

Facebook reporting system
www.facebook.com/help/?faq=12256

Twitter reporting system
support.twitter.com/forms/impersonation

Staff Sergeant Salvatore Giunta, Medal of Honor Recipient

Staff Sergeant Giunta was impersonated on Twitter before being awarded the Medal of Honor. The Online and Social Media Division reached out to Twitter and the imposter account manager to ensure it was identified as a "tribute" or "fan" account.

Case Study: Operational Environment

Social media in combat

There are multiple opportunities for strategic online engagement on several platforms in combat. Many deployed units maintain Facebook pages, Flickr sites and YouTube channels, for example.

Connecting from battle

More and more commanders see the value in using social media in combat. Social media can keep the public informed, it can keep Families connected and it can help address negative news stories and inaccurate reports.

CJTF-82 releases video of AH64 engaging
21,324 views - 2 years ago
3:08

CJTF-82

www.youtube.com/CJTF82Afghanistan

Combined Joint Task Force-82 in Afghanistan posted this video to their YouTube channel of an air weapons team engaging and killing insurgents who were attacking a small patrol base in Paktia Province. While the Taliban claimed Americans had killed innocent civilians, this video allowed CJTF-82 to accurately portray the actual event to the media and the world, thus correcting misinformation while building trust and confidence in the Army as an institution.

General Ray Odierno

www.facebook.com/RayOdierno

When it comes to using social media to compliment his outreach strategy, General Odierno has been an ambitious and enthusiastic leader. An early advocate, General Odierno maintains a vibrant and informative Facebook page. During his multiple tours in Iraq, Facebook was a ready source of information and an opportunity for discussion for his Facebook followers and other interested readers. His page provided updates from theater, keeping Family members connected during deployments. He continues to use Facebook on a regular basis.

Case Study: Garrison Crisis Management

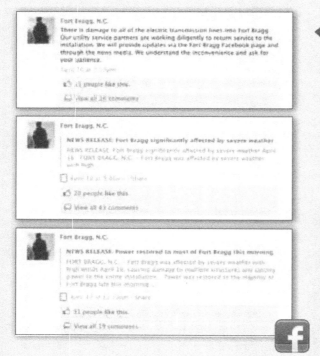

Fort Bragg tornado

On April 16, 2011, Fort Bragg was affected by severe weather with high winds, causing damage to multiple structures and cutting power to the entire installation. As a result, Fort Bragg was forced to close with the exception of key and essential personnel. It remained closed until power was restored to the installation. With the power down and the installation closed, it was difficult to get information out to the communities surrounding Fort Bragg. The installation turned to social media to disseminate information and provide updates. Once power was restored, Fort Bragg continued to use social media to document the efforts made to clean up the installation and get it back in working order.

The screen captures to the left and below are examples of messages and photo updates Fort Bragg posted to their Facebook page to keep the community up-to-date.

Case Study: Family Readiness

Social media and Army Families

Social media is becoming a valuable tool for keeping Families and Soldiers connected, which is vitally important to unit well-being. Family Readiness Groups (FRGs) are key organizations that reap the social media benefits by providing a venue for support, assistance and community resources. FRG social media sites have become the alternative to running from physical location to physical location to find out what is happening at an installation. They also provide discussion sections where the FRG, Soldiers and Families can post information and photos about installation news and activities.

What not to post?

- Specific unit movement information

- When/if a family is going on vacation or leaving the house vacant

- Gossip

- Information concerning MIA/KIA prior to release by DoD

What are good items to post?

- Pride and support for service, units, specialties and service member

- Generalizations about service or duty

- General status of the location of a unit ("operating in southern Afghanistan" as opposed to "operating in the village of Hajano Kali in Arghandab district in southern Afghanistan")

- Links to published articles about the unit or service member

- Any information already in the public domain

4th Brigade, 1st Armored Division FRG
www.facebook.com/4BCT1AD.FRG

The 4th Brigade, 1st Armored Division Family Readiness Group successfully uses Facebook page to inform Family members. It has announcements to keep Families up-to-date on activities of interest. Followers are very active and often post additional information to the posted announcements. The interaction on this page, much like other FRG pages is dynamic, interesting and informative. Newcomers to a unit can go to the unit's page to get answers to questions they may have about their new unit or location. Connecting online often eases the stress and anxiety or moving to a new unit.

Case Study: Army Leaders and Social Media

Leaders in action

The previous case studies illustrate how leaders around the Army have used social media in garrison and operational environments, but social media use goes much deeper than that. It is about the daily interactions and some of the Army's highest ranking leaders have tapped into social media platforms to communicate with the population at large.

Chief of Staff of the Army
www.facebook.com/CSADempsey
twitter.com/martin_dempsey

Chief of Staff of the Army, General Martin E. Dempsey is an advocate of social media. He actively uses the platforms to engage with various Army audiences by posting, commenting, Tweeting and responding to people who visit his sites.

Sergeant Major of the Army
www.facebook.com/SMAChandler
twitter.com/SMAChandler

Sergeant Major of the Army Raymond F. Chandler III uses Facebook to distribute new Army guidance and information to Soldiers worldwide. He also uses it to facilitate discussions about Soldier issues like training and uniforms.

Connecting with the public

Maintaining a social media presence is not limited to simply engaging on your own platforms. Some Army leaders have taken it a step further. In the example below, when it came to the attention of Vice Chief of Staff of the Army General Peter Chiarelli that a popular blog was reporting that Soldiers were wearing orange vests to identify them as suicidal, he was compelled to comment on the blog. By personally commenting on the blog, General Chiarelli changed the narrative, as did the blogger.

Reaching out

Leaders across the Army understand that social media in a new way to connect with various Army audiences. By reaching out through video, Facebook and blogs, Army leaders are engaging a new population of individuals who scour social media platforms for news rather than traditional media outlets. Social media helps bring the news to the user rather than forcing Army leaders to wait for the user to come to them.

Facebook Quick Reference Guide

DO:

- Start with a strategy – How does social media fit into your overall communication goals?
- Scatter your posts throughout the day, nights and weekends; do not clump all together
- Post on weekends and evenings, and evaluate which time works best
- Try to tag at least one other page in each post, when possible or appropriate
- Ask an engagement question for every post, when possible
- Respond to questions in a timely manner
- Post a comment policy and enforce it
- Remember to post in a friendlier tone, but not unprofessional
- Spell check every post prior to posting; the Army's reputation is at stake
- Thank your followers and praise them often
- Mix it up: photos, questions, videos, sharing others' content, news stories, etc
- Use lots of quality photos (be sure to add as many details about the photo as possible – or ask your audience to add details as an engagement item; also ask them to tag themselves or others)
- Use short, raw, catchy video
- Ask yourself: would I share that with my friends?
- Add a personal touch; connect with your audience
- Set defaults to show only your posts first (after all, this is a command information platform, and this allows your message to be seen first, and allows others to still comment on your wall)
- Welcome participation, collaboration and feedback
- Get a short, smart vanity URL (facebook.com/username) (available only after 25 followers)
- Update top 5 photos often (show a variety of activities, angles, personnel, etc)
- Have someone else read your posts before you post them (to see if they make sense)
- Track metrics and evaluate how content performs. Determine what metrics are important to you before you engage, set a benchmark and track over time.
- "Like" sister or similar organizations, and tag them often
- Post information or comments on other pages, while using your organization's page
- Always be mindful of OPSEC when posting
- Identify/find subject matter experts to answer questions that people ask on your page
- Avoid using automated posting services to post same content to multiple sites
- Ask your followers what they would like to see on the page
- List links to other sites, like Twitter and blogs, on the information tab

DON'T:

- Post too many times a day (you will lose followers)
- Clutter all your posts at one time or seem spammy
- Be too promotional
- Use boilerplate messages or snoozy press releases, unless necessary
- Use social media (teen) language in professional posts (ex: I wanna b ur bff 2day & 4evr)
- Use geotagged programs (ex: showing location where you are Tweeting or Facebooking)
- Post a link without giving some sort of lead, description or call to action
- Remove content just because you don't like it. If it doesn't violate your comment policy, leave it!

REMEMBER:

- You do not control what happens to a message once it is posted.
- It only takes one unprofessional slip to taint a reputation.
- If you do not have a lot of time to monitor, then set tighter restrictions (photos, videos, comments, etc).

Twitter Quick Reference Guide

DO:

- Be creative by posting different types of information
- Use URL shorteners (Google: http://goo.gl/ or Go.USA.gov: http://Go.USA.gov/)
- Use hashtags in every Tweet by searching for established hashtags and creating your own
- Tweet links to content (articles, photos, websites)
- Tweet breaking news related to your unit
- Tweet Army senior leader quotes
- Live Tweet events
- Create your own hashtags for events; explain and advertise these early and often
- Use Twitter to communicate during a crisis
- Follow other Army and DoD Twitter accounts
- Check often for new Twitter accounts and acknowledge, follow, share, etc
- Retweet content from other accounts while also adding your organization's words
- Engage with your Twitter audience by asking questions and retweeting their answers
- Include usernames of other accounts in your Tweets to boost awareness and followership
- Listen to what your followers are talking about
- Ask yourself "Would I want to retweet this?" before Tweeting
- Check your direct messages and mentions daily and respond
- Create a voice and personality for your organization
- Become the go-to resource for timely news and information
- Use direct messages to engage with your organization's followers
- Focus on Tweeting exceptional content
- Mix up your Tweet times
- Edit your Tweets and avoid typos
- Include a disclaimer (Following does not equal endorsement)
- Brand your page
- Include a link to official site in biography
- List Twitter page on your Facebook page
- Use Twitpics

DON'T:

- Tweet too many times in a day (you will lose followers)
- Clutter all of your Tweets at one time
- Follow brands (Pepsi, Coke, etc.) It looks like an endorsement
- Follow imposters or those with religious or political affiliation
- Obsess about the number of followers you have
- Tweet on the hour (everyone does that)
- Be too promotional
- Tweet with unprofessional Twitter language ("lol" "2 be" "OMG")
- Let your Twitter account become stagnant (go more than a week without Tweeting)
- Add location to Tweets
- Connect Twitter to Facebook or have automated Tweets with no engagement

REMEMBER:

- You do not control what happens to a message once it is posted.
- Once a Tweet is out there, it is out there.
- If you are Tweeting from a mobile device, be sure you do not mix professional and personal on the same device.

Frequently Asked Questions

Q: How do I get content on the Army's social media pages?
A: You can email stories, photos or links to unit videos to the Online and Social Media Division at ocpa.osmd@us.army.mil. We will work hard to feature them on our sites.

Q: I've never been on Facebook (Twitter, YouTube, etc). How do I get started?
A: First, know that you're not alone. Fortunately most social media platforms are relatively easy to use. The best way to get started is to find someone you know who is savvy with social media to show you the ropes. You can also start your own personal social media accounts so that you can familiarize yourself with how they work. The Online and Social Media Division also maintain Social Media resources for Facebook, Twitter and Blogs that are available on SlideShare (www.slideshare.net/USArmySocialMedia). If you have any questions that you can't find answers to you can always call the Online and Social Media Division or your local public affairs officer.

Q: Who can manage my unit's Facebook page?
A: Currently, social media manager is not an Army military occupation specialty, so it is often viewed as an additional duty. Often times, public affairs specialists take the role of social media managers since much of the content loaded to social media sites is news and command information. But it doesn't necessarily have to work that way. If a Soldier is motivated and the commander approves his/her managing the site, anyone can run a social media site as long as they work closely with the unit's public affairs shop in accordance with DTM 09-026.

Q: What if my unit doesn't have enough money or people to manage a social media presence?
A: Many social media platforms are free (Facebook, Twitter, YouTube, Flickr, etc), so it is possible to have a social media presence without a budget. Limited manpower does not limit your unit's ability to maintain a social media presence. Evaluate the platforms and determine which will work best for your manpower situation. It only takes one person to run a Facebook page and a Twitter account.

Q: Can I delete comments on my unit's Facebook wall?
A: Every registered social media presence in the Army is required to have a posting policy that should indicate what can and cannot be posted to a Facebook wall. If users violate these terms on your unit's wall, you are entitled to delete the comment and block the user if necessary. Keep in mind that Facebook is about facilitating the conversation so stick to your posting policy, but don't delete comments just because they express negative opinions about your organization.

Q: What are the elements of a Tweet?
A: A basic Tweet will typically have one of four main elements: a retweet or public reply, another Twitter handle (account name), a hashtag, and a shortened URL or link. Sometimes a Tweet will have all the elements like the example below.

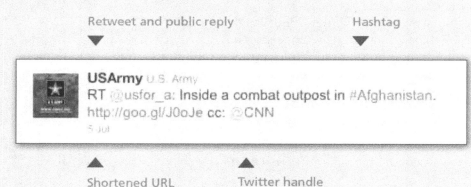

Retweet and public reply   Hashtag

USArmy U.S. Army
RT @usfor_a: Inside a combat outpost in #Afghanistan.
http://goo.gl/J0oJe cc: @CNN
5 Jul

Shortened URL   Twitter handle

Q: How can I increase the number of individuals who follow my unit on Facebook and Twitter?
A: Be creative. There is no surefire way to increase followers on Facebook and Twitter. Different techniques work for different organizations so it is important to think outside the box. Ask your followers to participate in the conversation, respond to them directly and ask them what they expect out of your social media presence. Look at what other organizations are doing. If they launch a successful campaign on Facebook, feel free to use their example and tailor it to your unit. Social media is still evolving so there is a lot of room to be creative. Don't be afraid to experiment and have fun.

Q: What happens if someone is impersonating me or someone in my unit?
A: Report the impersonation to the social media platform by clicking on the report button or emailing the platform directly. If the platform is unresponsive and the impersonation becomes a threat to reputation or personal safety, contact the Online and Social Media Division for assistance.

Q: Where should I direct recruiting related questions asked on my unit's social media profiles?
A: Army recruiting resources include goarmy.com, the goarmy.com Facebook page, @goarmy Twitter feed, goarmyvideos YouTube channel and ArmyStrongStories.com. The latter is an online community where Soldiers, supporters and families are blogging, sharing stories and answering questions about recruiting, as well as life in the Army.

Q: A family member posted something that violates OPSEC. What do I do now?
A: If the post is particularly offensive, the first thing you should do is take a screen capture of the post and delete it. It is also advised to engage that person in a discreet manner and explain that information isn't appropriate for conversation online. If the person posts again, you have the option to block them or report them. This should be used as a last resort because it is difficult to undo and only shifts the problem to out of view—the person will more than likely continue to post inappropriate content somewhere else. In either case, you should notify your command so that they are informed of the OPSEC breach and can take appropriate action.

Q: I did some searching and found that this command already has a non-official Family Group on Facebook (Twitter, YouTube, etc). What should I do?
A: Many commands have unofficial social media presences established by former Soldiers, Veterans or just fans excited about that command. We do not have the right to remove these presences nor would we want to unless they portrayed themselves as an official presence. In the meantime, work with the command leadership to determine if you want to approach the page and/or simply monitor it and chime in when you have information to add. You may also want to contact the administrator and touch base. These official presences are listed in the U.S. Army Social Media Directory which can be found at: www.army.mil/socialmedia. Temporarily, the Social Media Directory lists only command presences, not family readiness groups.

Q: I'm transferring my duties as the social media manager. What should I do?
A: If you established your social media presences under a general command account, it is as simple as turning over the login and passwords and teaching the new social media manager how the platform works. If you have been using your personal account to relay information, you will need to introduce the new social media manager on the social platform to the audience. Make sure to give the new social media manager administrator privileges.

Q: Should my organization use collaboration tools like milSuite, milBook and Intellipedia?
A: This social media handbook deals specifically with social media sites outside of the firewall. Consult your individual organization to determine how it uses these specific collaboration tools.

Official Army Social Media Presences
Managed by the Office of the Chief of Public Affairs | Online and Social Media Division

 defense.gov/socialmedia | Department of Defense Social Media Hub

 army.mil/blog | ARMY | LIVE - The Official U.S. Army Blog

 my.army.mil | Your Army Media. How You Like It.

 army.mil/mobile | U.S. Army Mobile Applications

 army.mil/features | Army.mil Web Features

 army.mil/create | Army Web Developer and Designer Creative Resources

 army.mil/standto | Daily Compilation of News and Information for Army Leaders

 army.mil/core | Army.mil Web Publishing and Content Management Platform

 facebook.com/USArmy | The Official U.S. Army Fan Page

 twitter.com/USArmy | The Official U.S. Army Twitter

 youtube.com/USArmy | The Official U.S. Army YouTube

 flickr.com/SoldiersMediaCenter | The Official U.S. Army Flickr

 vimeo.com/USArmy | The Official U.S. Army Vimeo

 slideshare.net/USArmySocialMedia | U.S. Army Social Media Resources

Social Media Resources

The Department of Defense and the Army have dozens of social media resources available for social media managers, Soldiers and their Families.

POLICY RESOURCES

☐ Standardizing Official U.S. Army External Official Presences (Enclosure 1)

☐ Delegation of Authority – Approval of External Official Presences (Enclosure 2)

☐ DTM 09-026 – Responsible and Effective Use of Internet-based Capabilities (Enclosure 3)

☐ AKO Social Media Portal: www.army.mil/suite/page/505262

OTHER SOCIAL MEDIA RESOURCES

☐ Army Social Media Directory: www.army.mil/socialmedia

☐ STRATCOM Social Networking Training: www.stratcom.mil/snstraining

☐ Interagency OPSEC Support Staff: www.ioss.gov

☐ Interagency OPSEC Support Staff Social Networking Training: goo.gl/AqmE1

☐ OnGuard Online: www.onguardonline.gov

☐ Anti-Phishing Phil: goo.gl/ZFkY3

Social Media Glossary: A – D

* This list is for situational awareness and is not all-encompassing. Listing terms does not equate endorsement.

A

Application Programing Interface (API): A documented interface that allows one software application to interact with another application. An example of this is the Twitter API.

Atom: Web feeds are used by the blogging community to share recent entries' headlines, full text and attached multimedia files. These providers allow other websites to incorporate the blog's "syndicated" headline or headline-and-short-summary feeds under various usage agreements. Atom also provides a standard way to export an entire blog, or parts of it, for backup or for importing into other blogging systems.

Avatar: An image or username that represents a person online within forums and social networks. The image to the right is the Army's avatar for its social media platforms.

Army Live Blog: The Army's official blog. www.army.mil/blog

B

Bit.ly: A popular free URL shortening service that provides statistics for the links users share online. Use it to condense long URLs and make them easier to share on social networks like Twitter. Use of bit.ly can be controversial due to rumors of its association with Libya. It is recommended that organizations use Go.USA.gov or Google URL shortener (http://goo.gl). www.bitly.com

Blip.TV: An online video sharing site. It offers both a free and a paid platform for individuals and companies who want to host an online video show. www.blip.tv

Blog: A word that was created from the two words "Web log". Blogs are usually maintained by an individual with regular entries of commentary, descriptions of events or other material such as graphics or video. Entries are commonly displayed in reverse-chronological order. "Blog" can also be used as a verb, meaning to maintain or add content to a blog.

Blogger: A free blogging platform owned by Google that allows individuals and companies to host and publish a blog. www.blogger.com

Blog Talk Radio: Blog Talk Radio is a free Web application that allows users to host live online radio shows. www.blogtalkradio.com

BoardReader: A free search engine that allows users to search for keywords only in posts and titles of online forums. www.boardreader.com

Box.net: A website that enables users to organize and view all of their content online in a familiar file and folder structure. Possibilities include sharing content with direct links to files and folders, turning any folder into a public Web page in one click, and creating widgets to share files on a company Web page or blog. www.box.net

Boxee: A social video application that enables users to watch online videos on their TVs and computers. Users can share and watch videos from a variety of online sources for free. www.boxee.tv

C

Chat: Any kind of communication over the Internet, but traditionally describes one-to-one communication through a text-based chat client commonly called an instant messaging application.

Collective Intelligence: A shared or group intelligence that emerges from the collaboration and competition of many individuals and appears in consensus decision-making in social networks.

Comment: A response that is often provided as an answer of reaction to a blog post or message on a social network. Comments are a primary form of two-way communication on the social Web.

Compete: A Web-based application that offers users and businesses Web analytics and enables people to compare and contrast the statistics for different websites over time. www.compete.com

Craigslist: A popular online commerce site in which users sell a variety of goods and services to other users. The reduction of classified advertising in newspapers across the United States has been attributed to Craigslist. www.craigslist.com

Creative Commons: A nonprofit corporation dedicated to making it easier for people to share and build upon the work of others, consistent with the rules of copyright. It provides free licenses and other legal tools to mark creative work with the freedom the creator wants it to carry, so others can share, remix, use commercially, etc.

Crowdsourcing: A combination of the words crowd and outsourcing, it refers to asking a question via social media and collecting answers from your various communities and users. The term has become popular with businesses, authors and journalists as shorthand for the trend of leveraging the mass collaboration enabled by Web 2.0 technologies to achieve business goals.

D

Delicious: A free online bookmarking service that lets users save website addresses publicly and privately online so that they can be accessed from any device connected to the Internet and shared with friends. www.delicious.com

Digg: A social news website that allows members to submit and vote for articles. Articles with the most votes appear on the homepage of the site and subsequently are seen by the largest portion of the site's membership as well as other visitors. www.digg.com

Disqus Comments: A comment system and moderation tool for a website or blog. It enables next-gen community management and social Web integrations to any site on any platform.

DocStoc: An online sharing service for documents. Users can view, upload, share and sell documents. www.docstoc.com

DropBox: A free service that lets you bring your photos, documents and videos anywhere and share them easily. www.dropbox.com

Social Media Glossary: E – I

E

Eventbrite: A website that provides online event management and ticketing services. Eventbrite is integrated with Facebook, so users can also promote their events there to drive more visits to their event page and sell more tickets. The service is free to use if your event is free; if you sell tickets to your event, there is a small fee per ticket. www.eventbrite.com

F

Facebook: A social networking website. Users can create a personal profile, add other users as friends, and exchange messages and profile updates. It is the world's largest social network with more than 600 million users (as of January 2011). www.facebook.com

Flash Mob: A large group of people who assemble suddenly in a public place, perform an unusual and pointless act for a brief time, then quickly disperse. The term flash mob is generally applied only to gatherings organized via social media, viral emails or phone.

Flickr: A social networking website centered around online picture sharing. The service allows users to store photos online and then share them with others through profiles, groups and other methods. www.flickr.com

Follow: A term used to describe how one receives information from social media sites like Facebook and Twitter.

Forum: An online discussion site (also known as a message board). It is the modern equivalent of a traditional bulletin board, and a technological evolution of the dial-up bulletin board system.

Formspring: A question-and-answer-based social website that allows its users to set up a profile page, from which anyone can ask them questions. www.formspring.me

Foursquare: A location-based social networking website, software for mobile devices, and also a game. Users "check-in" at venues using a mobile website, text messaging or a device-specific application — they're then awarded points and sometimes "badges." www.foursquare.com

FriendFeed: A real-time feed aggregator that consolidates the updates from social media and social networking websites, social bookmarking sites, blogs, as well as any other type of RSS/Atom feed. Users can create/share customized feeds of this information, as well as originate new posts/discussions/comments with friends. www.friendfeed.com

G

Google Buzz: A social networking and messaging tool from Google, designed to integrate into the company's email program, Gmail. Users can share links, photos, videos, status messages and comments organized in "conversations" and visible in the user's inbox.

Google Documents: A group of Web-based office applications that includes tools for word processing, presentations and spreadsheet analysis. All documents are stored and edited online, and allow multiple people to collaborate on a document in real-time.

Google+: A social networking service operated by Google Inc. The service launched on June 28, 2011 in an invite-only "field testing" phase. plus.google.com

Gowalla: A social network in which friends share their locations and connect with others in close proximity to each other. www.gowalla.com

H

Hashtag: Because Twitter provided no easy way to group Tweets or add extra data, the Twitter community came up with their own way: hashtags. A hashtag is similar to other Web tags — it helps add Tweets to a category. Hashtags have the 'hash' or 'pound' symbol (#) preceding the tag, like so: #socialmedia, #marketing, #hashtag.

hi5: A social network focused on the youth market. It is a social entertainment destination, with a focus on delivering a fun and entertainment-driven social experience online. www.hi5.com

HootSuite: A Web-based Twitter client for individuals and organizations. With HootSuite, you can manage multiple Twitter profiles, pre-schedule Tweets and view metrics, and teams can collaboratively schedule updates to Twitter, Facebook, LinkedIn, WordPress and other social networks via Web, desktop and mobile platforms. www.hootsuite.com

I

IceRocket: An Internet search engine which specializes in real-time search. It is generally used for blog searches but has expanded into searching the popular social networking websites Twitter and MySpace as well as news searches. www.icerocket.com

Impressions: An impression gives Facebook administrators a look at how many raw impressions an administrator initiated post on the Page received, as well as the overall feedback rate. These insights are aiming to help Page administrators understand more about the time of day, day of week, and type of content is most effective for delivering information to a fan base.

IntenseDebate Comments: A third-party commenting system for blogs. Custom integration with your blogging administrator panel makes moderation easy. Comment threading, reply-by-email, user accounts and reputations, comment voting, along with Twitter and FriendFeed integrations enrich reader experience.

Insights: Facebook Insights provides Facebook Page owners and Facebook Platform developers with metrics around their content. By understanding and analyzing trends within user growth and demographics, consumption of content, and creation of content, Page owners and Platform developers are better equipped to improve their business with Facebook.

Instant Messaging (IM): A form of real-time direct text-based communication between two or more people. More advanced instant messaging software clients also allow enhanced modes of communication, such as live voice or video calling.

Social Media Glossary: J – Q

J

Joomla!: An open source content management system (CMS) which enables users to build websites and online applications. Many aspects, including its ease of use and extensibility, have made Joomla popular. www.joomla.org

K

Kyte: An online and mobile video application that provides video hosting and stream for both recorded and live video feeds. www.kyte.tv

L

Lifecasting: A continual broadcast of events in a person's life through digital media. Typically, lifecasting is transmitted through the Internet and can involve the use of wearable technology.

Like: An action that can be made by a Facebook user. Instead of writing a comment for a message or a status update, a Facebook user can click the "Like" button as a quick way to show approval and share the message.

Link Building: An aspect of search engine optimization (SEO) in which website owners develop strategies to generate links to their site from other websites in hopes of improving their search engine ranking. Blogging has emerged as a popular method of link building.

LinkedIn: A business-oriented social networking site. LinkedIn had more than 100 million registered users in more than 200 countries. www.linkedin.com

Livestream: A live streaming video platform that allows users to view and broadcast video content using a camera and a computer through the internet. www.livestream.com

Lurker: A person who reads online discussions on a message board, newsgroup, social network or other interactive system, but rarely or never participates in the discussion.

M

Mashable: Founded in 2005, Mashable is the top source for news in social and digital media, technology and Web culture. With more than 50+ million monthly pageviews, Mashable is the most prolific news site reporting breaking Web news, providing analysis of trends, reviewing new websites and services, and offering social media resources and guides. www.mashable.com

Mashup: A content mashup contains multiple types of media drawn from pre-existing sources to create a new work. Digital mashups allow individuals or businesses to create new content by combining multiple online content sources.

MySpace: A social networking website owned by News Corporation. MySpace became the most popular social networking site in the United States in June 2006, but it was overtaken by its primary competitor, Facebook, in April 2008. www.myspace.com

N

News Reader: Enables users to aggregate articles from multiple websites into one place using RSS or Atom feeds. The purpose of these aggregators is to allow for a faster and more efficient consumption of information.

Newsvine: A social news site similar to Digg in which users submit and vote for stories to be shared and read by other members of the community. www.newsvine.com

O

Orkut: A social networking website that is owned and operated by Google. It is named after its creator, Google employee Orkut Büyükkökten. Although Orkut is less popular in the United States than competitors Facebook and MySpace, it is one of the most visited websites in India and Brazil. www.orkut.com

P

Pandora: A social online radio station that allows users to create stations based on their favorite artists and types of music. www.pandora.com

Permalink: An address or URL of a particular post within a blog or website.

Podcast: A non-streamed webcast; a series of digital media files, either audio or video, that are released episodically and often downloaded through an RSS feed.

Posterous: A blogging and content syndication platform that allows users to post content from any computer or mobile device by sending an email. www.posterous.com

PostRank: An aggregator that monitors and collects social engagement data related to content around the Web. It helps publishers understand which type of content promotes sharing on the social Web. www.postrank.com

Q

Qik: An online video streaming service that lets users to stream video live from their mobile phones to the Web. www.qik.com

QR Code (Quick Response Code): A specific matrix barcode (or two-dimensional code) that is readable by dedicated QR barcode readers and camera telephones. The code consists of black modules arranged in a square pattern on a white background. The information encoded may be text, URL, or other data.

Quantcast: A media measurement, web analytics service that allows users to view audience statistics (traffic data and demographics) for millions of websites. www.quantcast.com

Quora: An online knowledge market. Users ask and answer questions from other users, and read existing questions and answers. www.quora.com

Social Media Glossary: R – U

R

Real-Time Search: The concept of searching for and finding information online as it is produced. Advancements in search technology coupled with the growing use of social media enable online activities to be queried as they occur, whereas a traditional Web search crawls and indexes Web pages periodically and returns results based on relevance to the search query.

Reddit: A social news site similar to Digg and Newsvine. It is built upon a community of users who share and comment on stories. www.reddit.com

RSS (Really Simple Syndication): A family of Web feed formats used to publish frequently updated works — such as blog entries, news headlines, audio and video — in a standardized format. An RSS document (which is called a "feed," "Web feed" or "channel") includes full or summarized text, plus metadata such as publishing dates and authorship. Web feeds benefit publishers by letting them syndicate content automatically. They benefit readers who want to subscribe to timely updates from favored websites or to aggregate feeds from many sites into one place. RSS feeds can be read using software called an "RSS reader," "feed reader" or "aggregator," which can be Web-based, desktop-based or mobile-device-based.

S

Scribd: A social publishing site that turns document formats such as PDF, Word and PowerPoint into a Web document for viewing and sharing online. www.scribd.com

Second Life: An online virtual world. Users are called "residents" and they interact with each other through avatars. Residents can explore, socialize, participate in individual and group activities, create and trade virtual property and services with one another, and travel throughout the world.

Seesmic: A social software application site offering Seesmic Desktop, an Adobe Air application that integrates multiple Twitter accounts and your Facebook account and pages. Seesmic also offers a browser-based client for Twitter, a native Windows desktop client, and clients for mobile phones. www.seesmic.com

Sentiment: In the context of social media, sentiment refers to the attitude of user comments related to a brand online. There has been an explosion of free and paid social media monitoring tools that measure sentiment, including TweetMeme, HootSuite and PostRank, to name a few.

SlideShare: An online social network for sharing presentations and documents. Users can view files on SlideShare or embed them on other social networks. www.slideshare.com

Skype: A free software application that enables users to make video and voice calls, send instant messages and share files with other Skype users. Users can also purchase plans to receive phone calls through their Skype account. www.skype.com

Social Media Marketing: A term that describes use of social networks, online communities, blogs, wikis or other online collaborative media for marketing, sales, public relations and customer service.

Social Media Monitoring: A process of monitoring and responding to social media mentions related to a business or brand.

Social Mention: A free social media search and analysis platform that aggregates user generated content from across the Web into a single stream of information. www.socialmention.com

Streaming: A process of broadcasting media live over the Internet. It involves a camera for the media, an encoder to digitize the content, a media publisher where the streams are made available to potential end-users, and a content delivery network to distribute and deliver the content. The media can then be viewed by end-users live.

StumbleUpon: A free Web browser extension which acts as an intelligent browsing tool for discovering and sharing websites. www.stumbleupon.com

T

Tag Cloud: A visual depiction of user-generated tags or simply the word content of a site, typically used to describe the content of websites.

Technorati: A popular blog search engine that also provides categories and authority rankings for blogs. www.technorati.com

TweetDeck: An application that connects users with contacts across Twitter, Facebook, MySpace, LinkedIn and more. www.tweetdeck.com

Tweetup: An organized or impromptu gathering of people that use Twitter.

Twitter: A platform that allows users to share 140-character-long messages publicly. User can "follow" each other as a way of subscribing to each others' messages. Additionally, users can use the @username command to direct a message towards another Twitter user. www.twitter.com

Twitter Search: A Twitter-operated search engine that finds Twitter messages and users in real time.

Tumblr: A microblogging platform that allows users to post text, photos, videos, links, quotes and audio to their tumblelog, a short-form blog. www.tumblr.com

TypePad: A free and paid blogging platform similar to Blogger. It allows users to host and publish their own blogs. www.typepad.com

U

Unconference: A facilitated, participant-driven conference centered on a theme or purpose. The term "unconference" has been applied, or self-applied, to a wide range of gatherings that try to avoid aspects of a conventional conference, such as high fees and sponsored presentations.

Ustream: The leading live interactive broadcast platform that enables anyone with an Internet connection and a camera to engage their audience in a meaningful, immediate way. Unlike previous webcasting technology, Ustream uses a one-to-many model, which means that the user can broadcast to an audience of unlimited size. www.ustream.tv

Social Media Glossary: V – Z

V

Video Blog (vlog): A blog the produces regular video content often around the same theme on a daily or weekly basis. An example of a successful video blog is Wine Library TV.

Viddler: A popular video sharing site similar to YouTube and Vimeo in which users can upload videos to be hosted online and shared and watched by others. www.viddler.com

Vimeo: A popular video sharing service in which users can upload videos to be hosted online and shared and watched by others. Vimeo user videos are often more artistic and the service does not allow commercial video content. www.vimeo.com

Viral Marketing: A term that refers to marketing techniques that use pre-existing social networks to produce increases in brand awareness or to achieve other marketing objectives through self-replicating viral processes.

W

Web 2.0: Commonly associated with Web applications that facilitate interactive information sharing, interoperability, user-centered design and collaboration on the Web. A Web 2.0 site (e.g. Facebook) enables its users to interact with each other as contributors to the site's content, in contrast to websites where users are limited to the passive viewing of information.

Web Analytics: The measurement, collection, analysis and reporting of Internet data for purposes of understanding and optimizing Web usage.

Webcast: A media file distributed over the Internet using streaming media technology to distribute a single content source to many simultaneous listeners/viewers. A webcast may either be distributed live or on demand. Essentially, webcasting is "broadcasting" over the Internet.

Webinar: Short for Web-based seminar, a presentation, live meeting, training or lecture that is transmitted over the Internet. It is typically one-way, from the speaker to the audience with limited audience interaction, such as in a webcast. A webinar can be collaborative and include polling and question & answer sessions to allow full participation between the audience and the presenter.

Widget: An element of a graphical user interface that displays an information arrangement changeable by the user, such as a window or text box. Widgets are used on both websites and blogs.

Wiki: A website that allows the easy creation and editing of any number of interlinked Web pages via a Web browser, enabling collaboration between users.

Wikipedia: A free, Web-based, collaborative, multilingual encyclopedia project supported by the non-profit Wikimedia Foundation. Its 15 million articles (over 3.3 million in English) have been written collaboratively by volunteers around the world, and almost all of its articles can be edited by anyone with access to the site. www.wikipedia.org

WordPress: A content management system and contains blog publishing tools that allow users to host and publish blogs. This blog runs on WordPress and uses the Thesis theme. www.wordpress.com

X

Xing: A social software platform for enabling a small-world network for professionals. The platform offers personal profiles, groups, discussion forums, event coordination and other common social community features. www.xing.com

Y

Yammer: A business communication tool that operates as an internal Twitter-like messaging system for employees within an organization. It provides real-time communication and reduces the need for email. www.yammer.com

Yelp: A social network and local search website that provides users with a platform to review, rate and discuss local businesses. Over 31 million people access Yelp each month, putting it in the top 150 U.S. Internet websites. www.yelp.com

YouTube: A video-sharing website where users can upload, share and view videos. It is the largest video sharing site in the world. www.youtube.com

Z

Zoho: A suite of online Web applications geared towards business productivity and collaboration. www.zoho.com

Zooomr: An online photo sharing service similar to Flickr. www.zoomr.com

DEPARTMENT OF THE ARMY STANDARD OPERATING PROCEDURE ON
STANDARDIZING OFFICIAL U.S. ARMY EXTERNAL OFFICIAL PRESENCES (SOCIAL MEDIA)

DEPARTMENT OF THE ARMY
OFFICE OF THE CHIEF OF PUBLIC AFFAIRS
ONLINE AND SOCIAL MEDIA DIVISION
1500 ARMY PENTAGON
WASHINGTON DC 20301-1500

01 November 2010

SUBJECT: Standardizing official U.S. Army external official presences (social media)

1. References:
   a. Secretary of the Army Memorandum – Delegation of Authority – Approval of External Official Presences, 21 Oct. 2010
   b. Directive Type Memorandum DTM 09-026, Responsible and Effective Use of Internet Based Capabilities, 25 February 2010
   c. CIO/G6 Memorandum, Responsible Use of Internet Based Capabilities, 2010

2. The purpose of this memorandum is to standardize Army-wide External Official Presences (EOPs) (aka social media sites).

3. IAW Delegation of Authority memorandum (referenced above) commands are authorized to establish EOPs.

4. U.S. Army Family Readiness Groups may establish an official presence with the approval of their command. It is possible the unit's official page also serves the dual purpose as a platform for its Family Readiness Group to disseminate information, however, if the command elects to have separate pages they must adhere to the same standards.

5. All U.S. Army EOPs, to include pages on Facebook, Twitter, Flickr, YouTube, blogs and any other platform must adhere to the following standards:

   a. must be categorized as a government page
   b. include the Commander approved names and logos (i.e. 1st Brigade, 25th Infantry Division [Family Readiness]), not nickname nor mascot (i.e. not the "dragons")
   c. branding (official name and logos) across all social media platforms (i.e. Facebook, Twitter) are uniform
   d. include a statement acknowledging this is the "official [Facebook] page of [enter your unit or organizations name here] [Family Readiness]"
   e. Facebook pages must default to the "Just [your unit or organization's]" on the wall (Do this by selecting "edit page," then "manage permissions." Drop down under the "wall tabs page" and select "only post by page"). This results in command information being the first and primary thing on the wall, instead of spam and others comments.
   f. Facebook pages must include "Posting Guidelines" under the "Info Tab." Use the U.S. Army's Facebook policy as a reference and/or visit the DoD Social Media user agreement at: http://www.ourmilitary.mil/user_agreement.shtml
   g. be recent and up-to-date. Post must not be older than one month.
   h. adhere to Operations Security guidelines. FRSAs/FRG leaders should provide all page administrators and FRG members with the U.S. Army Social Media OPSEC presentation and the FBI Briefing on Identity Theft located on the U.S. Army's slideshare site at www.slideshare.net/usarmysocialmedia.

SUBJECT: Standardizing official U.S. Army external official presences (social media)
01 November 2010

    i.   should not be used as a place for personal advertisement nor endorsement
    j.   All pages must be registered through the U.S. Army at www.army.mil/socialmedia

6. The Office of the Chief of Public Affairs has the right to deny any page during the approval process if one or more of these guidelines are not followed.

7. For step-by-step instructions on how to set up pages, visit: http://socialmedia.defense.gov/learning-and-resources/training/social-media-guides/how-to-guides/ Further information, instruction, techniques, etc. can be found at www.slideshare.net/usarmysocialmedia

8. In order to sign up to receive weekly lessons, TTPs, etc. on how to manage social media pages, send an email to the email address below.

9. Use the platforms' help option to resolve questions, such as: http://www.facebook.com/help/ If questions are not resolved there, direct all questions and concerns to ocpa.osmd@us.army.mil.

10. POC for this memorandum can be reached at ocpa.osmd@us.army.mil

//original signed//
JUANITA A. CHANG
MAJ, CM
Director, Online and Social Media Division,
   Office of the Chief of Public Affairs

SECRETARY OF THE ARMY
WASHINGTON

SASA

2 1 OCT 2010

MEMORANDUM FOR SEE DISTRIBUTION

SUBJECT: Delegation of Authority – Approval of External Official Presences

1. References:

a. Deputy Secretary of Defense Directive-Type Memorandum 09-026, Responsible and Effective Use of Internet-based Capabilities, February 25, 2010.

b. CIO/G-6 Memorandum, Responsible Use of Internet-based Capabilities, March 25, 2010.

2. In accordance with reference a., I hereby delegate the authority to approve the establishment of External Official Presences (EOP) to the commanders of all Army Commands, Army Service Component Commands, Direct-Reporting Units; to the Director of the Acquisition Support Center; and, to the Chief of Public Affairs for Headquarters, Department of the Army and its Field Operating Agencies. EOP will be established in accordance with the standards set forth in the references above.

3. EOP are official public affairs activities conducted on internet-based capabilities. Internet-based capabilities are the publicly accessible information capabilities and applications available on the internet in locations not owned, operated, or controlled by the Department of Defense or the Federal Government. They include social networking services and other collaborative tools listed in reference a.

4. Unless expressly prohibited or restricted by law, directive, regulation, policy, or as set forth herein, the individuals specified in paragraph 2, above, may re-delegate this authority to a subordinate general officer or member of the Senior Executive Service within their organization. Any re-delegation of this authority may further restrict or condition a subordinate's exercise of this authority. No delegation or re-delegation of the authority conferred herein shall be effective unless it is in writing and determined not to be legally objectionable by the servicing judge advocate or legal counsel.

5. Record copies of delegations and re-delegations will be provided to the Office of the Administrative Assistant for archiving within ten days of taking effect. The individuals delegated to in paragraph 2, above, will remain responsible and accountable for all actions taken pursuant to this delegation of authority or any subsequent re-delegation of authority.

SASA
SUBJECT: Delegation of Authority – Approval of External Official Presences

6. This delegation is effective immediately and expires three years from the effective date, unless earlier suspended, revoked or superseded.

John M. McHugh

DISTRIBUTION:
Principal Officials of Headquarters, Department of the Army
Commander
    U.S. Army Forces Command
    U.S. Army Training and Doctrine Command
    U.S. Army Materiel Command
    U.S. Army Europe
    U.S. Army Central
    U.S. Army North
    U.S. Army South
    U.S. Army Pacific
    U.S. Army Special Operations Command
    Military Surface Deployment and Distribution Command
    U.S. Army Space and Missile Defense Command/Army Strategic Command
        Eighth U.S. Army
    U.S. Army Network Enterprise Technology Command/9th Signal Command (Army)
    U.S. Army Medical Command
    U.S. Army Intelligence and Security Command
    U.S. Army Criminal Investigation Command
    U.S. Army Corps of Engineers
    U.S. Army Military District of Washington
    U.S. Army Test and Evaluation Command
    U.S. Army Reserve Command
    U.S. Army Installation Management Command
Superintendent, U.S. Military Academy
Director, U.S. Army Acquisition Support Center

CF:
Director, Army National Guard
Commander, U.S. Army Accessions Command
Director, U.S. Army Office of Business Transformation

DIRECTIVE-TYPE MEMORANDUM (DTM) 09-026 – RESPONSIBLE AND EFFECTIVE USE OF INTERNET-BASED CAPABILITIES

DEPUTY SECRETARY OF DEFENSE
1010 DEFENSE PENTAGON
WASHINGTON, D.C. 20301-1010

February 25, 2010
Change 2, February 22, 2011

MEMORANDUM FOR: SEE DISTRIBUTION

SUBJECT: Directive-Type Memorandum (DTM) 09-026 - Responsible and Effective Use of Internet-based Capabilities

References: See Attachment 1

Purpose. This memorandum establishes DoD policy and assigns responsibilities for responsible and effective use of Internet-based capabilities, including social networking services (SNS). This policy recognizes that Internet-based capabilities are integral to operations across the Department of Defense. This DTM is effective immediately; it will be converted to a new DoD issuance. This DTM shall expire effective 1 ~~March, 2011~~ *January 2012.*

Applicability. This DTM applies to:

- OSD, the Military Departments, the Office of the Chairman of the Joint Chiefs of Staff and the Joint Staff, the Combatant Commands, the Office of the Inspector General of the Department of Defense, the Defense Agencies, the DoD Field Activities, and all other organizational entities within the Department of Defense (hereafter referred to collectively as the "DoD Components").

- All authorized users of the Non-Classified Internet Protocol Router Network (NIPRNET).

Definitions. Unless otherwise stated, these terms and their definitions are for the purpose of this DTM.

- Internet-based capabilities. All publicly accessible information capabilities and applications available across the Internet in locations not owned, operated, or controlled by the Department of Defense or the Federal Government. Internet-based capabilities include collaborative tools such as SNS, social media, user-generated content, social software, e-mail, instant messaging, and discussion forums (e.g., YouTube, Facebook, MySpace, Twitter, Google Apps).

- external official presences. Official public affairs activities conducted on non-DoD sites on the Internet (e.g., Combatant Commands on Facebook, Chairman of the Joint Chiefs of Staff on Twitter).

- official public affairs activities. Defined in DoD Instruction (DoDI) 5400.13 (Reference (a)).

Policy. It is DoD policy that:

- The NIPRNET shall be configured to provide access to Internet-based capabilities across all DoD Components.

- Commanders at all levels and Heads of DoD Components shall continue to defend against malicious activity affecting DoD networks (e.g., distributed denial of service attacks, intrusions) and take immediate and commensurate actions, as required, to safeguard missions (e.g., temporarily limiting access to the Internet to preserve operations security or to address bandwidth constraints).

- Commanders at all levels and Heads of DoD Components shall continue to deny access to sites with prohibited content and to prohibit users from engaging in prohibited activity via social media sites (e.g., pornography, gambling, hate-crime related activities).

- All use of Internet-based capabilities shall comply with paragraph 2-301of Chapter 2 of the Joint Ethics Regulation (Reference (b)) and the guidelines set forth in Attachment 2.

Responsibilities. See Attachment 3.

Releasability. UNLIMITED. This DTM is approved for public release and is available on the Internet from the DoD Issuances Website at http://www.dtic.mil/whs/directives.

Attachments:
As stated

DIRECTIVE-TYPE MEMORANDUM (DTM) 09-026 – RESPONSIBLE AND EFFECTIVE USE OF INTERNET-BASED CAPABILITIES

DTM 09-026, February 25, 2010

DISTRIBUTION:
SECRETARIES OF THE MILITARY DEPARTMENTS
CHAIRMAN OF THE JOINT CHIEFS OF STAFF
UNDER SECRETARIES OF DEFENSE
DEPUTY CHIEF MANAGEMENT OFFICER
COMMANDERS OF THE COMBATANT COMMANDS
ASSISTANT SECRETARIES OF DEFENSE
GENERAL COUNSEL OF THE DEPARTMENT OF DEFENSE
DIRECTOR, OPERATIONAL TEST AND EVALUATION
DIRECTOR, COST ASSESSMENT AND PROGRAM
    EVALUATION
INSPECTOR GENERAL OF THE DEPARTMENT OF DEFENSE
ASSISTANTS TO THE SECRETARY OF DEFENSE
DIRECTOR, ADMINISTRATION AND MANAGEMENT
DIRECTOR, NET ASSESSMENT
DIRECTORS OF THE DEFENSE AGENCIES
DIRECTORS OF THE DoD FIELD ACTIVITIES

ATTACHMENT 1

REFERENCES

(a)   DoD Instruction 5400.13, "Public Affairs (PA) Operations," October 15, 2008
(b)   DoD 5500.7-R, "Joint Ethics Regulation," August 1, 1993
(c)   DoD Directive 8500.01E, "Information Assurance (IA)," October 24, 2002
(d)   DoD Instruction 8500.2, "Information Assurance (IA) Implementation,"
        February 6, 2003
(e)   DoD Directive 5400.11, "DoD Privacy Program," May 8, 2007
(f)   DoD Directive 5230.09, "Clearance of DoD Information for Public Release,"
        August 22, 2008
(g)   DoD Manual 5205.02-M, "DoD Operations Security (OPSEC) Program Manual,"
        November 3, 2008
(h)   DoD Directive 5015.2, "DoD Records Management Program," March 6, 2000
(i)   DoD 5200.1-R, "Information Security Program," January 14, 1997
(j)   DoD 5240.1-R, "Procedures Governing the Activities of DoD Intelligence
        Components That Affect United States Persons," December 1, 1982
(k)   DoD Instruction O-8530.2, "Support to Computer Network Defense (CND),"
        March 9, 2001
(l)   Unified Command Plan, "Unified Command Plan 2008 (UCP)," December 17, 2008

THE UNITED STATES ARMY   SOCIAL MEDIA HANDBOOK

[43]

ATTACHMENT 2

GUIDELINES FOR USE OF INTERNET-BASED CAPABILITIES

1. <u>GENERAL</u>. This attachment applies to the official and/or authorized use of Internet-based capabilities by DoD personnel and all authorized users of the NIPRNET. Examples include, but are not limited to:

    a. SNS.

    b. Image- and video-hosting web services.

    c. Wikis.

    d. Personal, corporate, or subject-specific blogs.

    e. Data mashups that combine similar types of media and information from multiple sources into a single representation.

    f. Similar collaborative, information sharing-driven Internet-based capabilities where users are encouraged to add and/or generate content.

2. <u>OFFICIAL PRESENCES</u>. External official presences shall comply with Reference (a) and clearly identify that the Department of Defense provides their content. In addition, external official presences shall:

    a. Receive approval from the responsible OSD or DoD Component Head. Approval signifies that the Component Head concurs with the planned use and has assessed risks to be at an acceptable level for using Internet-based capabilities.

    b. Be registered on the external official presences list, maintained by the Assistant Secretary of Defense for Public Affairs (ASD(PA)), on www.Defense.gov.

    c. Comply with References (a) and (b) as well as DoD Directive (DoDD) 8500.01E, DoDI 8500.2, DoDD 5400.11, DoDD 5230.09, DoD Manual 5205.02-M, DoDD 5015.2, DoD 5200.1-R, and DoD 5240.1-R (References (c) through (j), respectively).

    d. Use official DoD and command seals and logos as well as other official command identifying material per ASD(PA) guidance.

e. Clearly indicate the role and scope of the external official presence.

f. Provide links to the organization's official public website.

g. Be actively monitored and evaluated by DoD Components for compliance with security requirements and for fraudulent or objectionable use (References (d), (g), and (i)).

3. OFFICIAL USE. Official uses of Internet-based capabilities unrelated to public affairs are permitted. However, because these interactions take place in a public venue, personnel acting in their official capacity shall maintain liaison with public affairs and operations security staff to ensure organizational awareness. Use of Internet-based capabilities for official purposes shall:

a. Comply with References (b) through (j).

b. Ensure that the information posted is relevant and accurate, and provides no information not approved for public release, including personally identifiable information (PII) as defined in Reference (e).

c. Provide links to official DoD content hosted on DoD-owned, -operated, or -controlled sites where applicable.

d. Include a disclaimer when personal opinions are expressed (e.g., "This statement is my own and does not constitute an endorsement by or opinion of the Department of Defense").

4. RECORDS MANAGEMENT. Internet-based capabilities used to transact business are subject to records management policy in accordance with Reference (h). All users of these Internet-based capabilities must be aware of the potential record value of their content, including content that may originate outside the agency.

5. LIMITED AUTHORIZED PERSONAL USE. Paragraph 2-301 of Reference (b) permits limited personal use of Federal Government resources when authorized by the agency designee on a non-interference basis. When accessing Internet-based capabilities using Federal Government resources in an authorized personal or unofficial capacity, individuals shall employ sound operations security (OPSEC) measures in accordance with Reference (g) and shall not represent the policies or official position of the Department of Defense.

DTM 09-026, February 25, 2010

<u>ATTACHMENT 3</u>

<u>RESPONSIBILITIES</u>

1. <u>ASSISTANT SECRETARY OF DEFENSE FOR NETWORKS AND INFORMATION INTEGRATION/DoD CHIEF INFORMATION OFFICER (ASD(NII)/DoD CIO)</u>. The ASD(NII)/DoD CIO, in addition to the responsibilities in section 4 of this attachment, shall:

    a. Establish and maintain policy and procedures regarding Internet-based capabilities use, risk management, and compliance oversight.

    b. Provide implementation guidance for responsible and effective use of Internet-based capabilities.

    c. Integrate guidance regarding the proper use of Internet-based capabilities with information assurance (IA) education, training, and awareness activities.

    d. Establish mechanisms to monitor emerging Internet-based capabilities in order to identify opportunities for use and assess risks.

    e. In coordination with the Heads of the OSD and DoD Components, develop a process for establishing enterprise-wide terms of service agreements for Internet-based capabilities when required.

2. <u>UNDER SECRETARY OF DEFENSE FOR INTELLIGENCE (USD(I))</u>. The USD(I), in addition to the responsibilities in section 4 of this attachment, shall:

    a. Develop procedures and guidelines to be implemented by the OSD and DoD Components for OPSEC reviews of DoD information shared via Internet-based capabilities.

    b. Develop and maintain threat estimates on current and emerging Internet-based capabilities.

    c. Integrate guidance regarding the proper use of Internet-based capabilities into OPSEC education, training, and awareness activities.

    d. Ensure that all use of Internet-based capabilities that collect user or other information is consistent with DoD 5240.1-R (Reference (j)).

3. <u>ASD(PA)</u>. The ASD(PA), in addition to the responsibilities in section 4 of this attachment, shall:

    a. Maintain a registry of external official presences.

    b. Provide policy for news, information, photographs, editorial, community relations activities, and other materials distributed via external official presences.

    c. Provide guidance for official identifiers for external official presences.

4. <u>HEADS OF THE OSD AND DoD COMPONENTS</u>. The Heads of the OSD and DoD Components shall, within their respective Components:

    a. Approve the establishment of external official presences.

    b. Ensure the implementation, validation, and maintenance of applicable IA controls, information security procedures, and OPSEC measures.

    c. Ensure that computer network defense mechanisms that provide adequate security for access to Internet-based capabilities from the NIPRNET are in place, effective, and compliant with DoD Instruction O-8530.2 (Reference (k)).

    d. Educate, train, and promote awareness for the responsible and effective use of Internet-based capabilities.

    e. Monitor and evaluate the use of Internet-based capabilities to ensure compliance with this DTM.

    f. Coordinate with USD(I) regarding the use of all Internet-based capabilities that collect user or other information, to ensure compliance with Reference (j).

5. <u>DoD COMPONENT CHIEF INFORMATION OFFICERS (CIOs)</u>. The DoD Component CIOs shall:

    a. Advise the ASD(NII)/DoD CIO and ensure that the policies and guidance for use of Internet-based capabilities issued by ASD(NII)/DoD CIO are implemented within their Component.

    b. In coordination with Component OPSEC and Public Affairs offices, provide advice, guidance, and other assistance to their respective Component Heads and other

DIRECTIVE-TYPE MEMORANDUM (DTM) 09-026 – RESPONSIBLE AND EFFECTIVE USE OF INTERNET-BASED CAPABILITIES

DTM 09-026, February 25, 2010

Component senior management personnel to ensure that Internet-based capabilities are used responsibly and effectively.

c. Assist their respective Component Head to ensure effective implementation of computer network defense mechanisms as well as the proper use of Internet-based capabilities through the use of existing IA education, training, and awareness activities.

d. Establish risk assessment procedures to evaluate and monitor current and emerging Component Internet-based capabilities in order to identify opportunities for use and assess risks.

e. In coordination with the Component Public Affairs Office, assist their respective Component Head in evaluating external official presences' intended use.

6. <u>COMMANDER, UNITED STATES STRATEGIC COMMAND (CDRUSSTRATCOM)</u>. The CDRUSSTRATCOM, in addition to the responsibilities in section 4 of this attachment, shall:

a. In accordance with Unified Command Plan 2008 (Reference (l)), direct the defense and operation of the DoD Global Information Grid (GIG).

b. Assess risks associated with the use of Internet-based capabilities, identify operational vulnerabilities, and work with the ASD(NII)/DoD CIO to mitigate risks to the GIG.

Notes

SOLDIER. CIVILIAN. SELF.
THERE ARE NO SPLIT PERSONALITIES IN SOCIAL MEDIA.

WWW.ARMY.MIL/SOCIALMEDIA

Blogs

Facebook

Twitter

Flickr

YouTube

Vimeo

Army Social Media